everyday
words

illustrated by Gaynor Berry

Ladybird

My body

eyebrow

mouth

ear

chin

lip

neck

hair

eye

cheek

nose

tongue

teeth

wash

eat

skip

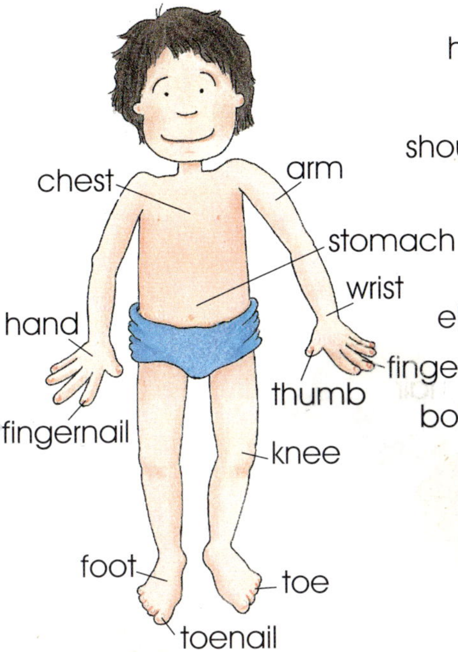

head

shoulder

chest

arm

stomach

wrist

hand

finger

fingernail

thumb

knee

elbow

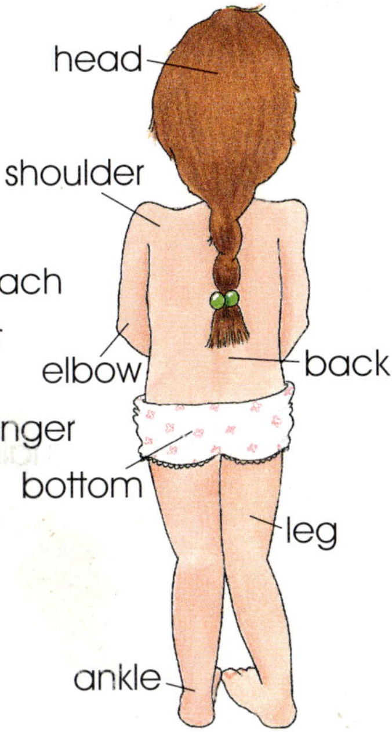

back

bottom

leg

foot

toe

ankle

toenail

yawn

tumble

sleep

Clothes

shorts

pyjamas

blouse

scarf

mittens

shirt

trousers

dress

tie

sweater/
jumper

sandals

boots

slippers

gloves

nightdress

vest

skirt

cardigan

coat

anorak

tights

jacket

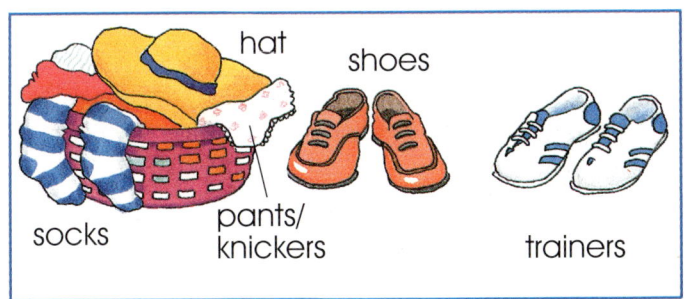

hat

shoes

socks

pants/
knickers

trainers

Families

grandad/grandpa

granny/grandma

wife

husband

sister

brother

baby

6

uncle   aunt   twins

cousin

mother/mummy   son   father/daddy

daughter

Food

milk

biscuits

chicken

beefburger

ham

eggs

juice

bread

salad

sausages

sauce

cheese

pizza

sugar

spaghetti

meat

sandwiches

jam

fruit

coffee

vegetables

orange

peas

yogurt

water

cake

apple

tea

nuts

orangeade

Everyday things

envelope

fire

fruit

butterfly

flowers

clock

hammer

bottle

camera

comb

apron

glass

iron

bath

bag

jug

apple

bricks

door

house

doll

box

chair

jar

More everyday things

kettle

leaf

moon

lamp

scissors

picture

paints

watch

table

stars

tin

mirror

television

keys

oven

sun

soap

tools

refrigerator

telephone

ribbon

pencils

book

wheelbarrow

The countryside

fence

forest

insects

cave

ladybird

bridge

river

hill

bees

fields

grass

leaf

worm

sky

windmill

waterfall

tree

mole

snail

hot air balloons

wasps

spider's web

orchard

lane

butterfly

gate

nest

caterpillar

flowers

bird

Doing words

dress

sit

read

write

wash

dry

sing

eat

walk

ride

drink

run

paint

yawn

dance

splash

creep

blow

wave

whisper

jump

cook

smile

shop

Animals

mouse

fish

crocodile

goat

gorilla

cat

lion

turtle

yak

koalas

snake

rabbit

whale

dog

octopus

frog

ducks

wolf

zebra

swan

sheep

panda

tiger

monkey

elephant

penguin

rhino

polar bear

People

explorer

pilot

nurse

actor

optician

dentist

workman

mechanic

detective

florist

baker

doctor

gymnast

canoeist

acrobat

driver

deep-sea diver

juggler

decorator

artist

astronaut

astronomer

butcher

Transport

boat

ambulance

motorcycle

tractor

jeep

aeroplane

helicopter

canoe

racing car

digger

bicycle

submarine

car

train

Shapes and colours

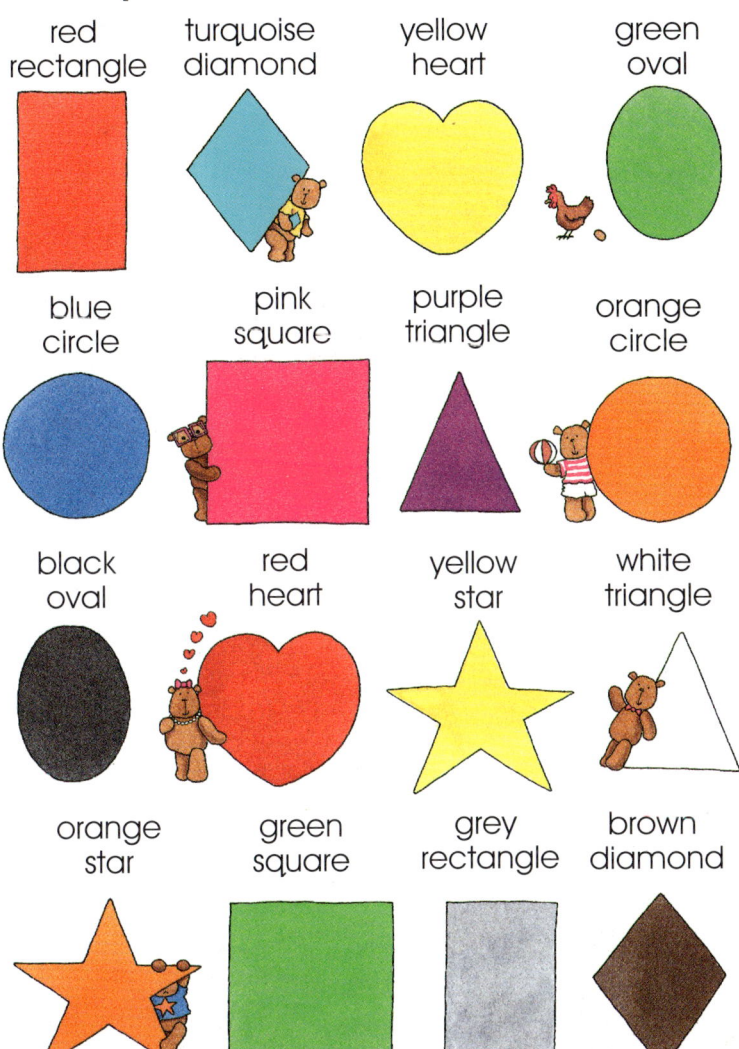

red
rectangle

turquoise
diamond

yellow
heart

green
oval

blue
circle

pink
square

purple
triangle

orange
circle

black
oval

red
heart

yellow
star

white
triangle

orange
star

green
square

grey
rectangle

brown
diamond

Numbers

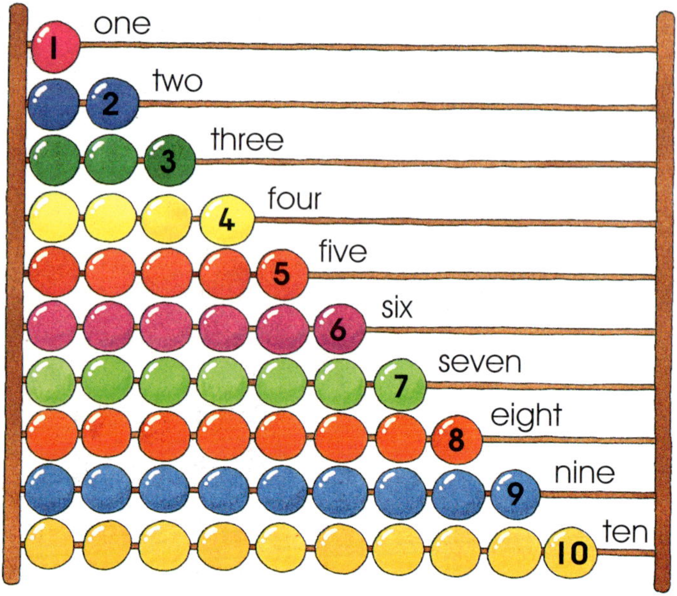

one 1
two 2
three 3
four 4
five 5
six 6
seven 7
eight 8
nine 9
ten 10

eleven	11	twenty one	21	
twelve	12	thirty	30	
thirteen	13	forty	40	
fourteen	14	fifty	50	
fifteen	15	sixty	60	
sixteen	16	seventy	70	
seventeen	17	eighty	80	
eighteen	18	ninety	90	
nineteen	19	one hundred	100	
twenty	20			

Weather words

snow

rainbow

sun

rain

thunder and lightning

Days of the week

Sunday
Monday
Tuesday
Wednesday
Thursday
Friday
Saturday

Months of the year

January
February
March
April
May
June
July
August
September
October
November
December

Opposite words

up

hot

cold

down

old

new

dirty

clean

thin

fat

tall

short

on

off

sad

happy

big

little

light

heavy

fast

slow

Words we write a lot

a
about
after
all
am
an
and
are
as
at
away

back
be
because
but

came
can
come

comes
coming

did
do
doing
down

for
from

get
getting
go
goes
going
good
got

had

has
have
having
he
her
here
him
his

I
if
in
into
is
it

like
look
looking